MW01121772

Ash & Embers

The Poiema Poetry Series

Poems are windows into worlds; windows into beauty, goodness, and truth; windows into understandings that won't twist themselves into tidy dogmatic statements; windows into experiences. We can do more than merely peer into such windows; with a little effort we can fling open the casements, and leap over the sills into the heart of these worlds. We are also led into familiar places of hurt, confusion, and disappointment, but we arrive in the poet's company. Poetry is a partnership between poet and reader, seeking together to gain something of value—to get at something important.

Ephesians 2:10 says, "We are God's workmanship . . ." *poiema* in Greek—the thing that has been made, the masterpiece, the poem. The Poiema Poetry Series presents the work of gifted poets who take Christian faith seriously, and demonstrate in whose image we have been made through their creativity and craftsmanship.

These poets are recent participants in the ancient tradition of David, Asaph, Isaiah, and John the Revelator. The thread can be followed through the centuries—through the diverse poetic visions of Dante, Bernard of Clairvaux, Donne, Herbert, Milton, Hopkins, Eliot, R. S. Thomas, and Denise Levertov—down to the poet whose work is in your hand. With the selection of this volume you are entering this enduring tradition, and as a reader contributing to it.

—D.S. Martin
Series Editor

Ash & Embers

Poems

JAMES A. ZOLLER

CASCADE *Books* • Eugene, Oregon

ASH & EMBERS
Poems

The Poiema Poetry Series

Cascade Books
An Imprint of Wipf and Stock Publishers
199 W. 8th Ave., Suite 3
Eugene, OR 97401

www.wipfandstock.com

PAPERBACK ISBN: 978-1-5326-3610-3
HARDCOVER ISBN: 978-1-5326-3612-7
EBOOK ISBN: 978-1-5326-3611-0

Cataloguing-in-Publication data:

Names: Zoller, James A.

Title: Ash & embers : poems / James A. Zoller.

Description: Eugene, OR: Cascade Books, 2018 | Series: The Poiema Poetry Series.

Identifiers: ISBN 978-1-5326-3610-3 (paperback) | ISBN 978-1-5326-3612-7 (hardcover) | ISBN 978-1-5326-3611-0 (ebook)

Subjects: LCSH: subject | subject | subject | subject

Classification: CALL NUMBER 2018 (paperback) | CALL NUMBER (ebook)

Manufactured in the U.S.A. 02/12/18

For the women in my life

my mother, in memoriam

my daughter and

my daughters-in-law, strong accomplished women all

my granddaughters with confidence and prayers

and for Donna, my past my present my future

vital as the next breath

Contents

HARD COPY

In Medias Res

If you ever climb the map again
you could stop there and whisper a few hymns

William Stafford, "Living on the Plains" [1993]

I was ashamed to ask the king for a band of soldiers and horsemen
to protect us against the enemy on our way, since we had told the king,
"The hand of our God is for good on all who seek him . . . ."
So we fasted and implored our God for this,
and he listened to our entreaty.

Ezra 8:22–23 [ESVUK]

In Medias Res

The poet regards the mirror formed by words
of his own making, and what he sees is fracture, reflections
that appear variously as trees and water;
as topography lined and chaotic with isobars;

as moments that vanish when they appear;
as the faces of his children or of others
who become his children; as the angelic
face of his beloved, honored in medias res;

as – in its own obsessive gravity – the face
behind the face he shows the world; as
– in flashes – as if he had somehow caught the sun –
burning glimpses of God that blind him

that bring him fumbling back to study its
depths. And to sing. Again. And again.

Photographs

and I was young and I heard sheepbells far off
a breeze in the almonds a voice
with its echo and a girl singing somewhere
and I thought it might be enough

W.S.Merwin, "Can Palat"

I divested myself of despair
and fear when I came here.

Jane Kenyon, "Notes from the Other Side"

The wind you walk against but do not feel is ignorance.

William Stafford, "12 September 1981,"
Every War Has Two Losers

Antebellum Family Photograph (1939)

One need not move to be in motion.
A breeze tugs at hems – skirt and pant leg drift.

A lock of disciplined hair is teased loose,
a gust makes the body lean against it

just as one leans against the future.
One need not move to be in motion.

The sun, too, misbehaves, crimping the eyes,
flashing on glass. Throwing its hard shadows.

So one comes to the black and white of 1939
not nearly as surprised as they were, captured

in their happy pose, disarmed by wind and sun,
– the world spinning madly but in some larger frame –

disarming in their attitudes. One need not move
to be in motion. In that photograph

lines and life remain vivid, while time
bumps us along, out of control.

His War

My father returned from that war
in a cloud of radiant dust.

In the days of the Empire's setting sun
his troop ship steams to port in its afterglow.

His war – the story he carried inside
but never told. Never explained. Silence
absolute, a cancer, as if his story like Japan itself
had been shredded, vaporized, cindered
in holocaust. Sun, unleashed.

Now we assemble the pieces of his war,
the skeletal trees, the oily pools
the sudden aging, the blasted lungs. How,
born on the wind, shall that story unfold?

Reconstructing Collective Memory

I can't speak for others
but my own rough scraps
of collective memory,
my handful of details, drop away
steadily in the dusk.

The memories I keep are soiled
by the worry
of my hands. I hope
for better from you,
but I suspect you are –
like me – inattentive.

Thus, the big questions
cannot be answered alone.

I show you my ideas.
You can show me yours.
We can hope we still hold enough
between us to figure out
who we are. What this all means.

Or to figure out
what pieces have slipped away.

Still, these I set between us
on the table of common interest
like so many pebbles,
as my witness,
polished now and dark.

Wyoming, 1952

When I was a small child
when seat belts were a luxury, unsought,
my older brothers took the window seats
while I hung forward into the grownup space
my feet on the hump down the center of the floor.

This is how I learned what I needed
about survival, about us, about the natural order,
Father behind the wheel, Mother reading maps,
comfortable talk passing like fence posts
ordinary as sage brush.

Just a still point in the rushing panorama.
For all I knew I could be anything I might imagine
aiming along the hood's raised spine
down the straight black highway
that opened into the future a mile a minute

reaching all the way to a horizon
always just a few more giant strides ahead.

Long Shadows

Distinct in its improvisations, an old memory
of late afternoon sun finding its notch
in the mountains west of Laramie
pauses there for one beat, one contraction –

the long shadows of the peaks
wrap the earth in their black fingers

until all that rises above the soil
that clings by roots and foundations
that hugs dirt with its belly
sinks in the shadows as into water.

And all that doesn't, all that transcends,
turns royal blue, or bronze, the sun itself
pulling back from across the open sky
until it too slides, suddenly, from sight –

and I let out my breath. After all that cosmic pageantry,
I see it blooming, radiant in darkening air.

And I turn toward familiar yellow windows,
warm rooms full of voices, comfort, and food.

My Grandfather's Hand

By the end he addressed envelopes from edge
to edge, at a forward slant precisely suited
to the matronly school mistress who had disciplined
his boyishness, who watched from over his shoulder –
like a predator – his orphaned hand.

The perfect loops and paralleled spikes
of my grandfather's textbook cursive held
for eighty years – growing large as if bold-
ness were a remedy for failing eyes, a trembling pen,
a dangerously erratic heart.

He varied not a whit – even in the grip
of his last illness – as if, still, to please her
whose stern attentions were as close as he
might ever imagine to a mother's.

Another Occasion

Accept this from me
as you might accept
on another occasion
a small, dried fish
from the hand of an old man.

You are in his kitchen
sitting at his bare table.
It is clean after
the fashion of old men.

Sunlight rides to the floor
on motes of dust.
The fish, on a small plate.
You must be hungry,
he urges, *please eat.*

Accept this from me:
Twenty years after his death
my father appeared
in a dream. He stood
at the back of a church
I knew from childhood
in light grainy with years.

In his narrow tie he looked
as I remembered him.
I could not speak.
Nor did he, though
his face held, perhaps,
the trace of a smile.

And when I awoke
with light from the full moon
sifting through the window
onto my face – I felt
that it was OK, that I could
go on. I felt
I could be somebody.

Life and Metaphor

Quiet as Tears

in the distance a dog barks
at the sound of a door closing
and at once I am older

W.S. Merwin, "Ancient World,"

What did I know, what did I know
of love's austere and lonely offices?

Robert Hayden, "Those Winter Sundays"

From the Moon

If we say that blue
is the color of water viewed from the moon
then blue is the color of life

and if we say that green
is the spectrum of life on land
and brown is land itself, arid perhaps
but home

and if we say that white
is the color of clouds, white being
as close as we get to atmosphere
to spirit

we might think that absolutes exist
that this view through open space
of earth is life, is breath
crossing the face of the deep

we might think we are crossing
the great void, mystery itself,
toward God

we might think it possible
to understand longing, to forgive loss,
to know the large grip
of love

The Natural Order of Things

Daughter, my world
revolves around yours:
            the earth
circles the moon
You are not impressed
with the natural order of things

It is six a.m.   It has
become familiar for me to work
with you on my lap
in these hours when the only sound is of rain
hitting the roof or pipes popping with heat
in the lower part of the house

Now
your slender panting
the slurp of your thumb

(to think I once found
my own pulse distracting)

As I work around
you, daughter, and your brother
who sleeps

the world is still
it is the sun that creeps

The Physics of Time

What we know about time
we know from the scars it leaves,
from its abiding confusions.

Like a mirror, time is impossibly thin,
a surface one cannot pass through,
a plain that allows us measure.

The present stares back.
So we dress up what we can see.
We prod and arrange.

There now. Wasn't that easy?
The present corrupts any soul
that desires its own beauty.

Truisms aside, what would time
mirror if not our saddest features,
our struggles with our human condition?

In fact, we *do* know something of the future:
The future is what appears
when we forget ourselves,
when we turn away.

Alchemy

When the sun drops
behind the hills
rimming this place where
you are, it slips
finger by finger from the stark
trees.

Soon you are
immersed in shadow –
an entire bowl of hill-shade –
where you wait
watching as snow
gathers the smothering dark
to its featureless
whiteness

and becomes not grey
as if all values were neutral,
born of black and white,
but something *other* – more
like love
or the gravity of planets –
transcendent

blue.

Toward a Birthday Poem

Now, older,
a thing apart,

May you never say
in your heart:

I shall visit
Father's house.

Where I live is
your house.

Here is the door
you never need open:

Whenever you care to
come in.

Why We Rehearse

Once
you imagined this day,
thought a cousin was bridegroom enough.
Another cousin attended.

Your gowns trailed badly,
train and hem, dragging fore and aft,
tripping your small feet, slid
to the toes of grandma's glossy shoes –

the unfilled, elevated heels
clack-clacking like tack hammers
against the hard tiles
of her broad front hall.

Such grand processions, gown
slid down your thin shoulders,
the thin tune of pomp and circumstance
from your own too-red lips.

Once
you imagined other parts
as they *ought* to be, who
stands where, with whom,

what to say, even how
it should be said –
step and turn and speak,
a little louder, please, but somehow

defer . . . until your cousin
who wasn't, yet,
groom enough himself
lost interest and wandered . . .

We have taken photographs
to hold against this day.
It is but one image I describe.
Once when we imagined

we failed to imagine
beyond that day.
But we prayed.
And when we prayed

with clacking heels and too-red lips
coming again and again to mind . . .
when we prayed,
we prayed toward this moment,

not for shoes that fit
or makeup properly managed
but for your own deep happiness
and for the man who *would be* groom enough.

Marriage: Prelude, Mystery, & Riddles

1.

stars dim
hearts waken.
toward morning
fog settles over Busan.
beneath a sliver of moon
a rose corona lies upon the hills.

2.

as from three
one
so from two
one
such divine math
the mystery of marriage
embodied
our most obvious
oneness

3.

So –
what is
male and female
divine and human
trinity and duet and singularity?

why must
harmony
demand all
mind heart body spirit
earth and eternity?

who would find
whole-ness
in the other,
as one,
finds
completion
in God.

Seamless Love

It is the genius of every young man
to feel in and of his young woman
that here he has found something
never before seen, heard, thought, felt,

that this gift which is this young woman
is more precious by far than any gift
ever given in mankind's wonderful
sad history, beyond even the dark

wonders of self awareness. And it
is the gift of every young woman
to feel in and of her young man
that her genius lies in giving her self

to this one who is new and strong
and faithful and her exact other.

Silence and Light: A Last Full Measure of Devotion

Received wisdom holds that translation
shifts between meaning and music.

Precision is what I mean. Original intention, that
sloppiest of motives. The grinding

of gutturals smoothed over millennia
in the rocky stream-bed of history itself.

So, we conclude according to our logic,
translation is less than the pristine *other*;

it is distortion, its face and hands disfigured,
grating on the ear, that portal to the soul.

If the poem is a three legged dog,
what creature can translation be?

It is all reduction anyway, a part
for the whole, voices for the inexpressible.

Take such wisdom to the chopping stump
and lay the axe to it. Unless it is a mirror –

or anesthetic for the soul – in its effort
to shoulder all of time and human suffering

each poem offers just itself, a keyhole
at which one kneels and peers.

What might one say of the grip of any moment?
Just this: In the middle of a cold November night

I am holding my granddaughter, red and battered
within an hour of birth. I have never seen

her before, yet my heart bangs about my chest.
Everything but this girl lies beyond the light.

Intrusions

Collateral Damage

When all the men of war are shot
And flags have fallen into dust,
Your cross and mine shall tell me still
Christ died on each, for both of us.

Thomas Merton, "For My Brother, Missing in Action 1943"

Some questions you would ask of God prove you unfit for God's company.

William Stafford, *Every War Has Two Losers*

News from the Front

This morning when bombs explode in Baghdad
and Iraqis kill more civilians than enemy
to send their confusingly blunt messages,
the language that accounts for the bodies
and waves the bleeding off in wailing ambulances,
the language that shapes what we see
is the language of our good intentions.

So this is what our good efforts have come to:
the obvious has been rendered obvious.

How wrenching
on any imaginable scale – the ruined cities,
the burned and mangled lorries,
black smoke billowing above the palms near the river,
bodies that may be civilians may be combatants
pulled from wreckage by ordinary brown hands
float in plain coffins above an angry crowd.

We have been at this battlefield before,
in a different foreign language. How did we forget?

We have known this moment before:
Whatever direction we look, *we know*
a people at war with itself.

Progress

Maps show elevations,
ground features, water sources.

Satellite cameras render details:
hard against soft, heat for light.

Computers enhance bits and bites
to bring them closer. All detail

is of great consequence.
The brown eyes, the two-day stubble,

the serial number on your weapon.
Soon we will grow software

to anticipate body language,
to tell us the color of a man's heart,

the intentions in his skull.
Soon we will say

send us everyone who imagines
he could have been guilty.

What Changes/What Stays the Same

Perhaps you remember a uniform
and a smart look – my hair,
which had not begun to thin,
cropped close to my head
leaving its brown roots –
a neat field, as it were,
all the sun-yellowed wanderings pruned away.

Perhaps I spoke.
But words, too,
drop away.
Even from the best memories. Sometimes,

the sun blazed as I stood in the snapping shadow
of a flag. Perhaps that is what you remember –
how that man suited the picture.

Now, if we can make space for sympathy –
that is, if we can *stand together* –
look with me a moment
at the field, newly cut,
row upon row of neat stubble.

Look closer. Rogue stalks remain.
Water stands in furrows from recent rains –
we will not work it any time soon.

We might bring the dead to bury here.
We have field enough. But don't call it *home*.
And these dead, clearly, belong to us. We knew them.
We sent them away.

But time alters. We should know.
Dying makes all things foreign.

A Story is More Than its Ending

We drive to the edge of town, my son and I, where
a handful of mashed and mangled cars sit in the yard of a body shop.

Beyond the shop, nearly hidden, is a house, a double-wide.
All else is corn field, tall dried-out stalks rustling in the breeze.

Stark images are possible here, dramatic black and white photographs
when the sun carries an edge. It will make your body *tingle.*

Just now this November morning the sun creeps onto the horizon.
In this hard light shadows stretch long and deep like claw marks.

Nothing is spared these clean lines and edges.
Stay here, I say to my son as I get out. He would rather sit anyway,

listening to the radio. I speak to the owner of the shop, who
seems glad to talk though he has more work than he can handle.

Keeps me busy, he says. *Sure, take pictures,* he says, *I have*
nothing to hide. We laugh. *Wrecked cars. Unharvested corn.*

A mess. Take all the pictures you have the patience for.
But he balks at rolling one wreck onto its roof.

It's personal, I say. *My son plowed his car through a corn field.*
We found it belly up, tires spinning. He walked away.

I smile. It's a long story, long in the telling. Happy ending.
We stand for a time, generally facing each other, quiet.

The light changes. It softens and flickers, now filtered
by the high thin clouds that reflect across the man's face.

He doesn't speak, although his mouth works to form
whatever needs to come next. *It's not your concern,* he says,

but my son didn't walk away.
So here we are, two fathers with different son stories.

A story is more than its ending. *The war, you know,* he says.
He says, *Sure, turn the car over if it helps,*

and he goes back into his shop where the car bodies lie.
Not today, I tell my son when I return.

The sun. We have lost our clean edges.

One Day While Laughing

So it happens this way: One day
while you are laughing with a friend
the heart gives out and you slump away.

If you are fortunate your chair holds you
until help, which is too late anyway, arrives.

The laughing has turned to *Oh, No*
and the great babble of What-to-Do.

But its already too late, as we know,
and the one with training uses it
on one no longer with us.

Now everyone will have stories to tell.
For sure it has ruined everyone's evening.

Except yours, oddly. This is why:
Because, despite the shock, the fuss,
the spectacle that you never wanted,

it all seems less urgent now.
And now that you have exited the door

that has caused so much anxiety
you know the hard part, the *not-knowing*, is over.

The Old Politics

When I speak, my words
are small weights
shifting the scale of talk –

perhaps because every –
thing I see I have seen before,
perhaps because I know that every
word laid on the scale carries
tipping weight. Or none at all.

Some days I think
it is all good. Every-
thing works out.

Other days are dark clouds
gathering on the horizon.
Why, I wonder, can't people
see what is happening here?
Why choose
ignorance, oblivion, black holes?

I am so old now that
I talk in this way.
What I sense is not so different
from what a boy at seventeen feels –

the future closing in, night
growing darker, the alley
smelling of urine and garbage,
an alley he has entered
but fears he cannot leave.

Grieving

As if the bodies lay about the room
Grotesque in their gestures, in their unearthly stillness,
Blood spattered on the walls, pooled on the floor,

The raw animal smell of bodies relieved of fluids
Shifts instantly to the putrific,
The busyness of dying.

As if you were there, it takes your breath.
It rings in your ears, it pounds pounds
In your chest, in your temples.

When I am asked to explain, I say nothing.
Or I say 'I hold the war inside me.
Without permission it feeds, it feeds on itself.'

Memory Loop

This is a short story
that repeats itself.
It is called Honor.
It is called Duty.

The soldier, long past
battle, perhaps,
lays the uniform out upon the bed
hat jacket blouse tie trousers socks shoes medals
as he was taught –
mother or basic training,
no matter.

This is short
a story that repeats
drawn from uniform
jacket socks shoes
solid somber colors
set out to assemble on his torso and limbs
one by one
flat plains smoothed
creases lined up just so
sharp straight symmetrical.

The man inside
trying hard to fill it out
to embody
what can no longer be
embodied.

This is a story
shorter
than expected
The smart soldier
assembled in the mirror
returns his salute
tremors un-reflected.
This sadness
is shorter
than expected.
The barreled salute
behind the brow
A sharp snap

This story dis
solves hat blouse
trousers red
red uniform red
blood to the floor
folds upon itself crumpled and honorably held together

This story repeats repeats
repeats re
peats

Certain Fictions

Growing up among sudden fires
weakens the eyes,

the brilliant bombs flashing
beyond my window flashing again

later, on the retina, destroying
sleep. And the sudden

words between my parents
like the searing arc of a welder

before I turn my face.
It is wartime in Europe

though it could have been anywhere.
Now in numbing midlife

after a night of snow
I go out to find myself

blinded, weeping in the dazzling sun.
It is always this way –

the world white, new; me, staggering,
though I no longer dream

of war. As for my parents,
even a blind man

can feel the rough welds
that have held them together.

Veteran

On the evening of the first missile
streaking into the night with its blazing tail,
John forgot how to sleep.

For days he sat
watching infra-red fireworks showering Baghdad,
live TV fusing with the endless loops of old film,

the same jet launching from the carrier's deck,
its engines' immense torches,
the same line of tanks racing into the desert, raising dust,

the same cross-hairs locking on one blip,
on one truck, on a long ribbon of highway.
Then the dark obliterating flash.

Sometimes in the night John would leave the screen
to stare at the darkness of the picture window.
For several days he showered, shaved, ate with his family

as if he were going to work, though work had become
this war, its stories, troop movements, precision
bombing, embedded reporters, body counts.

As if he were there, the smell of explosives, the stench
of the battlefield which is the stench of death, acrid smoke
of burning oilfields, burning tanks, burning sand

filled his head until he could not eat. His nausea was
a jungle nausea, the TV screen an open window, obliterating
flashes of napalm, carpet bombing. Banality of body bags.

A veteran himself, John's boss told Mary
Let's give it time to work itself out.
I'll hold his job. A mercy if the war is short.

Then a doctor prescribing sedatives for sleep
said *deserts are not jungles, but he's there just the same.*
And the stench gets lodged like a virus in the brain.

Anti-aircraft tracers blipped the blue screen like sonar.
TV news hounds hunkered in hotel rooms, small flares
light up the horizon, a red MUTE icon floats like flak.

John covers his ears, clenches his eyes.
He trembles. Stays put. War continues. A trail of tears
scores the geography of his cheeks like wadi.

When the Emperor was God

For thirty years after that incandescent sun, rising forever now,
consumed the wood and paper town of Hiroshima,

and rising again from the crowded alleys of Nagasaki,
Lieutenant Hiroo Onoda ignored the ruin of time and silence.

He held the mountain against such odds, awaiting words
that might have freed him from the tyranny of diligence.

The jungle's daily conversation joined macaw and screeching monkeys
but never the crackle of the wireless, never a commanding voice.

So it was that in this world grown unspeakably modern and
prosperous beyond imagining, Hiroo Onoda was discovered,

not by enemies of the Incarnate Sun for whom one's blood is duty
come to purge the island, but by a graduate student, who had fled

the tedium of yellowing records in dusty archives for the purely academic
adventure of time travel, who hunted Onoda down and in plain Japanese

persuaded him to sacrifice his burnished sword and his last
measure of devotion to an Emperor now so humanly dead.

Grief Comes by Pairs

My sons are of an age to soldier now.
Time has burdened me with father's cares.
I see the length of row before I plow.

One labors, as with oars, to guide the prow.
One grits and grins for what each moment bears.
My sons are of an age to soldier now.

I've shouldered what I must. A furrowed brow,
Grizzled hair – my days the coming winter pares.
I sense the length of row before I plow.

Chaos and commotion, a rendered sow,
The serpent coils, my anguished prayers.
My sons are of an age to soldier now.

I learn from where I've been, as times allow.
I carry on as strength permits and muscle wears.
I smell the turn of soil before I plow.

Remember: God's domain is *why*, man's is *how*.
Though death may come alone, grief comes by pairs.
My sons are of an age to soldier now.
I feel resistance in the earth before I plow.

Significant Chatter

Mere seconds before the clamor of crows
calls my eye across waves of muffling white,
it drops. As if the sky might deliver
perfect death, silent, sudden, it plummets, then
chaos – those black and furious wings that
follow its ominous ghost-like shadow
flying fast along the river bed, swooping
low beneath the snow-crusted walking-bridge,

emerging majestic, solemn, a snowy owl
skims downstream, slanting, effortless, swift.
But for the diminishing fuss and clatter of the crows
it flies undetected, rounds the bend scant
inches above the frozen snowy rapids
and is gone – a grey squirrel flagging in its talons.

Prayers & Conversations

Looking for God is the first thing and the last,
but in between such trouble, and such pain.

Jane Kenyon, "With the Dog at Sunrise"

Some nights, although we are faithless, the truth
enters our hearts, that small familiar pain;
then a man will stand stock-still, hearing his youth
in the distant Latin chanting of a train.

Carol Ann Duffy, "Prayer"

Sister Poem

Life happens,
is.

Poem becomes
– a separate thing.

Life and Poem
resemble Art,

share a father,
drift apart.

Poem takes
life's shoes,

walks in rain.
One strives

to resist Life's
bitterness,

to embrace both
– itself an art –

to reconcile
what grows apart.

A Hush at Westminster

Why should I have been surprised to find our dead gathered here
beneath the floor, their names and titles etched for the ages in stone,

obliterated now by time and season, by the shuffling of the faithful.
The more fortunate dead – interred strangely within the walls –

saved the humiliation of pilgrim feet, the slow wearing-away of features.
And those few, dignified, repose in crypts, their stony death masks

staring blindly at the vaulted shadows of heaven. The sanctuaries
are crowded now with so much death. Even here, where it all stops,

the striving after prominence. Though we, the living, are spared
the shame of seeing remains, it is clear what remains

of desire and ambition. All, all alike, in desperate need
of mercy.

Dis–quiet Mournful Hour

in my hours of darkness
I have eddied into prayer

O mournful commotion of soul
toward that great dark where God is

space and object and motion and above all
gravity in my dark

hours I have drifted
in soulful commiseration

with the God who is
above all in these hours

my thoughts fly as
light from the billion

unreachable stars communing
above and beyond all

reason but this gravity
object motion dark space

reaches at unimaginable
interval my blinking mind's eye

as embers and above all
my darkness my grubbing my

prayers in those sleepless
mourning hours I lie

in darkness waiting God what
gravity I am listening

Military Science

The day my son survived his roll-over
I caught a glimpse of what a father might feel
when *the notice* arrives.

It really doesn't matter whether it is hand delivered
or whether the gold on the letterhead is genuine.
I would have but one question.

When that question is answered I will have others.
Believe me I will have a lifetime of questions
that beg for answers.

But when I heard his voice and I went down to pick him up
I lost interest in the car the insurance the red tape
all that ungodly paperwork.

Time Stands Arrested

Today we work
in the dry hours
before the clouds,
darkening the mid-day sky,
reach critical mass
and the rain starts.

A few drops
sting shoulder and head
then a steady rain
sounding on leaves like wind
as we load rake
and hoe and
wheel the barrow
into the shed.

The leaves sigh,
then, serious drumming
on the shed roof,
the cold drops
burning into scalp and shirt.

That is all.

We watch from the gloom
just to the dry side
of sheets pouring
from the overhang,
astonished at the bright
water from heaven,
the rain chorus.

Time stands arrested
in that dream moment,
the world altered.

The Question of Peace in Our Time

Luminous flakes fall through darkness,
drift as only snow — or ash — is able, unhurried,
over empty streets, spreading a kind of peace,
as if peace might descend, evenly, muting the darkness.

I stir the fire to life when I arise in the banked hours
looking for sleep, for a semblance of rest, and find
coals beneath the ash of the evening's blaze glowing still,
eager to be coaxed to flame with slender dry sticks.

Low flames flicker along edges where an axe
has split the log, opening its heart, a ragged fire line,
the restless flame mesmerizing, soothing. I watch as one
watches surf, insensibly, an ineffable resonance.

When, in the pre-dawn, the brute plow rends the snow,
I have not slept. Nor am I able. The flames become coals
again, the soothing dance reduced to ash and embers.
Daylight marshals its forces. It will soon be upon us.

Prayer for All

Father, Christ, and Holy Ghost
Lift us from our dormant muddle

Take away our blinded egos
Grant reprieve from worthlessness

Grant us lives of adoration
Give us measure, give us pace

Take away our witless sinning
Strip away our need to control

Christ be Son and God be Father
Righteousness be His alone

Notes on Writing, Notes on Reading, A Few Odd and Well-Ordered Things

Because we write we know the cost
of every day

William Stafford, "A Poet to a Novelist"

On Reading Seamus Heaney

As I wander in among the poems
it takes a dark moment for my ears
to adjust to rhythms and tones
in voices, the way eyes go blind
in darkness and gradually learn again to see.

There is no rushing it. Some
remain blind, always. Or deaf. Then
as leaf shapes emerge from the dark sky
and the way forward opens just beyond
my feet, I find myself humming, talking back.

So it is, once upon a time, in medias res,
that the pulse and pitch echo somehow
in my own dark places and I find
my own words tumbling about, raised
by sympathetic vibrations.

The Argument

So what did you think when you picked up the book?
That you could read a lifetime of poems like a novel?

Nothing could be more perverse. A poem,
if it is any good, is like the point of a plow.

You, my friend, and I are unbroken fields, plain dirt.
In its first motion the poem catches and digs.

Each word cuts to depth and each line
pulls us forward until the furrow is opened.

What do we expect but opened ground?
The poem trades on old ideas. Still,

one must remember that none of us is more
than a few breaths removed from the soil.

Consider your hands, or how you examine clouds,
the way your face grows dark under the sun.

Consider how the field arranges itself along the furrow,
the torn and broken bread you lift, absently, to your tongue.

In Due Course

I look up words that come to mind
when I need a verb or a noun,
something to be or to hold, something moving.

I cradle the fat word-book, ledger, dense history,
and flip pages until my fingers grow warm,
then lay my head among inky shadings to listen.

Hearing, I find, is more accepting than sight.
Accurate is a clear cold stream, of course,
but nuance and variation are a feathered chorus.

I would have context and implication.
I would feel how stresses, like shadows, fall.
I would absorb, all told, what insinuates meaning,

the noises in the background, the smell of wet leaves
– not so much to trap what moves, as to trust.

On Reading Mao's Poems

Following old trails, Chinese poetics,
We speak of all things big and small as one,
As one character. One bold radical
Denotes time, peace – like the wings of a moth.

This moment in this ordinary room is
Like every moment in every cold room,
Timeless and plain – as if, through drawn curtains
In a corner opposite a closed door,

A breeze made heavy with melting snow . . .
Noon-high-sun descending through parting clouds . . .
Lives, faceless, hard as hand-to-hand combat . . .
Serene as red flags, a million bloody feet . . .

Old myth, you offer no consolations
Though your hand extends like the hand of God.

Second Knowings

Every image embodies a way of seeing.

John Berger, *Ways of Seeing*

Economies of Latitude

In the damp grey light
I sit on a low beach chair
on a deck my hands built
in the summer of my daughter's marriage.

The golden finches and the black-eyed junco
hop along the feeder edge, swoop in
and out, assert and displace,
feed together and flee.

A woodpecker somewhere beyond
bangs his dinner knocker
against an old infested pine.

A nuthatch skitters across the bark.

I do not envy the young
their hurry. I wait
with book and pen
for the sun to burn its hole
along the leafy horizon.

Perhaps a dozen voices in this morning choir,
as distinct as they are cacophonous,
having their moments as I
am having mine. It is a matter
of economies.

Now the cardinal shows

with her brighter mate.

A humming bird
has come to inspect me,
drab vegetation in a wonder-
land of fragrant and promising blossoms.
I follow the heavy buzz
of her hoverings as she lingers –
shifts left – then right,
now left again and gone.

As she sometimes does
to satisfy her curiosities
and her hungers
she hovers just here
to see me
face to face
as if to close the gap between us.

Life Map

My brothers, two before and two after,
are pins in the map. They value their own coordinates.

This has been true long enough for me to realize
that the valuable terrain lies under foot.

My mother and father were once pins, too,
in a village called *Here, Now*. I called it *Where I Am*.

Then my father vanished into the foothills,
having pulled loose somehow.

I imagined for a time he had become a mountain
or maybe a ridge above timber line he had once surveyed.

Now I imagine a range of rugged peaks
in the Wyoming Rockies. Snow smokes up to show us where.

My mother, too, is vanishing, but more slowly.
She is a meadow. Beyond is the salt marsh.

Then the sea. Gulls distract us with their cries.
Nowhere that can be fixed with a pin.

Beneath my feet is just the dirt I stomp around in.
When did I begin to watch the sky for signs?

I am full of ideas about territory yet ahead,
where the soil is new, that needs mapping.

Another Kind of Courage

-for our children, born and borrowed

1

These children born of us have gone
from belly to knees, from staggerings to steps.

They wander off, make lives,
bear children of their own.

And we – as fits our station – watch them go,
turn, come around. For blood and love they will

and do return. We watch and, thus, we grow.
Our sorrow lies in aging. And our joy.

2

Now children born of others fill our rooms.
Come nearly grown, they study us as they would books,

to learn us, as one learns to measure nouns and verbs,
or how to fold the hands, where eyes may go,

to find in face and voice a way to see themselves —
and we, in turn, to see our-selves in them.

What may be foreign once can be no longer.
How quickly blunders are forgiven, love returned.

3

All too soon we send them on their way.
Blood will not bring them back, though love remains.

Our sorrow lies in more than growing old; this loss is real.
Would we have acted otherwise, given what we know?

Rather, ask what pain or sorrow saved
outweighs each child, born or borrowed?

What we have done, we would again.
Though tender consolation, this must be enough:

to know that you are in the world still,
that you may choose well, and be happy.

Kaleidoscope

One eyed, yes. And one eye
sees the visual organ music
in that rose of nine petals,
nine-point celestial compass, a fine
odd number though not seven, not *perfection.*

Random, the number of luck,
nine is another math entirely –
a trinity of trinities, three squared,
an image shaped illuminated leveraged,
the *mandala,* tool of spectral navigation.

So I pulled off its smiling head
its single-eyed smiley-face its life-filter its rose-
colored glasses, only to discover
a petri dish with random shapes and shards
vivid, odd, and polished glass

the kind one might mistake for trash
– the kind one might liken
to chaos of the human soul,
the hit-or-miss of the universe,
the cluttered proofs for God.

Mapping the Hometown

Someone on the town council was progressive, visionary.
The future was not time but growth. With so many miles
of empty pavement, how could growth be anything but good?

So began the lining of roads. In all my old stomping grounds
bewildered houses abut the fast, crowded two-lanes,
their companionable stairs, stoops, short drives

become a danger to themselves, isolated by traffic,
withdrawn, clenched, afraid. Kids, renting second floor
walk-ups, fill old farmhouses again, park in paved barnyards.

So growth has come to this: We leave town to shop
along the roads between. No need for sidewalks.
Spaces open in town, then grow desolate, wild.

The Telling is All

He had his say. I have had mine,
nearly. The rest is details.

Now the children gather at the table,
all grown up, toting babies, watching

toddlers in that distracted way,
bearing debts, scars of teen rebellions

overcome, vague miseries
compressed into volatile rage

for that quiet one, things not planned,
uninvited guests. I have

had my say. I have lived my life. Let
the children speak.

Truth is in the telling –
let them set the record straight.

The Memory Test

On the morning of mom's evaluation
I want to think of other things,
not of what we might learn, nor of her fears
that life has turned, trees gone barren.

It is mid-October. Already
snow has buried many just north of us,
dark hours outnumber light hours.
Each day we lose a handful of minutes.

She has been afraid of losing yesterday,
this morning. I have been afraid
of losing my childhood, whatever
she has held for safe-keeping.

She knows my voice still,
and Sunday she drives her friends
– widows all – to dinner after church,
though there are fewer now to remember.

And the name of the restaurant. Well . . .
when I phone I ask of other things
– her weather, her friends. I report my news,
more great-grand-children on the way.

She knows how to know
our distance, those five hundred miles
the mountains in between, the rivers.
She knows to brush aside my concern.

Then she raises the issue I have avoided
– or rather her fears do. She wants to prove
how sharp she is still, but she fails
to name her sons' birthdays, her own test.

What science offers to tell us
reads like a calendar, or like a weather map.
Over time, we can watch the isobars
converge. We note the red Highs, the blue Lows.

But we have always known about winter.
Frost visits valleys; snow, the hill tops.
Leaves, having astonished us again . . .
Science will only confirm what we know.

But there is beauty, yet, in winter.
Let us not turn away.

Hard Copy

All Poems Are a Foreign Tongue

Spruce, inadequate, and alien
I stood at the side of the road.
It was the only life I had.

Jane Kenyon, "Three Songs at the End of Summer"

I have no way of telling what I miss
I am only the one who misses it

W.S. Merwin, "After the Voices"

Tai Chi

In October
when holly berries
glow red
in diminishing sun

their forest leaves
grow hard
and their spines
find the finger's quick

This is hard to say
remembering spring
how quickly the eye desires
how easily the fingers bleed

To Make of Them Grave Souls

We have told these stories before
as if rehearsing some bigger event
that will make sense of suffering.

Now as I tell my tale, arranging
its details for maximum effect, suspense
or empathy, your lips begin to move.

Your own story has already begun
in your mind, competing with and
shaping the story I am telling.

This is the ancient conversation
we each imagine we have invented.
Like one's personal discovery of sex,

we say here it begins and there,
there it ends, to give weight
to the characters and the story line,

so mundane, so timeless,
and, though it never really ends,
so perfectly engaging.

Shooting Accident

on my knees in the shallow snow
I strain to topple
the instant the bullet burst
and the belly tears to let it enter
I think how long I have had
to live in pain

blood runs in one thick black river
toward the earth's center
toward some strange man
it knew before me

already, I think as I lay down beside it
how terribly deep the snow is

Guarding Ounces At the UPS Desk, 1980

-for Frank

Because the scale works by mirrors
aligned between dim, distant light
and a dusty view-hole

Because boxes often overlap the tray
poorly bound
blocking vision

Because the floor shakes from trucks in the yard
from presses and stitchers on the second-floor assembly
from footfalls and the rattle of conveyors

Because it is a natural defect of the universe
for paper to disintegrate for hair to fall out
for the calculation of weights to defy logic

Because light is unreachable and suspect

Because debris obstructs

Because what one reads and accepts
is an image
of an image
of distant scales and vectors

Because one must, finally,
disregard the obstacles

Prayer For All

为所有人的祷告
(Chinese translation by Wei Hu)

圣父，基督，圣灵

将我们从休眠和困惑中提起

带走我们的盲目自我

赐饶恕给我们尽管不配

赐我们崇拜的生命

给我们步伐，给我们步调

带走我们的愚笨犯罪

除去我们控制的意念

基督是儿子, 上帝是父亲

义属于他一个人

In This End is Our Beginning

In these last days before the earth hardens
into its last malleable posture
we wake to find our small world
dappled with snow, its textures
far richer for the white dustings
than the forgetting snows of December.

This is a world we know
even as we learn its contours anew.

Hour by hour as the weakening sun
draws its warming brush wherever
it is not obstructed, the landscape
reemerges, glistening, renewed
even as it dries, its small wonders
beneath our feet quiet as tears.

… # Acknowledgements

"My Grandfather's Hand," published in *Tennessee English Journal*, 2003

"When the Emperor Was God," published in *di-Verse-city Anthology 2017*, Austin International Poetry Festival

"Shooting Accident" published in *Simple Clutter*, 1998

"Guarding Ounces at the UPS Desk," published in *Nadir*, 1983

COLLECTIONS IN THIS SERIES INCLUDE:

Six Sundays toward a Seventh by Sydney Lea

Epitaphs for the Journey by Paul Mariani

Within This Tree of Bones by Robert Siegel

Particular Scandals by Julie L. Moore

Gold by Barbara Crooker

A Word In My Mouth by Robert Cording

Say This Prayer into the Past by Paul J. Willis

Scape by Luci Shaw

Conspiracy of Light by D. S. Martin

Second Sky by Tania Runyan

Remembering Jesus by John Leax

What Cannot Be Fixed by Jill Peláez Baumgaertner

Still Working It Out by Brad Davis

The Hatching of the Heart by Margo Swiss

Collage of Seoul by Jae Newman

Twisted Shapes of Light by William Jolliff

These Intricacies by Dave Harrity

Where the Sky Opens by Laurie Klein

True, False, None of the Above by Marjorie Maddox

The Turning Aside anthology edited by D.S. Martin

Falter by Marjorie Stelmach

Phases by Mischa Willett

Second Bloom by Anya Krugovoy Silver

Adam, Eve, & the Riders of the Apocalypse
anthology edited by D.S. Martin

Your Twenty-First Century Prayer Life by Nathaniel Lee Hansen

Habitation of Wonder by Abigail Carroll